Congressional
Research
Service

Individual Income Tax Rates and Other Key Elements of the Individual Income Tax: 1988 To 2013

Gary Guenther
Analyst in Public Finance

February 1, 2013

Congressional Research Service

7-5700

www.crs.gov

RL34498

CRS Report for Congress

Prepared for Members and Committees of Congress

Summary

Statutory individual income tax rates are the tax rates that apply by law to various amounts of taxable income. Statutory rates lay the foundation for marginal and average effective tax rates, which most economists believe have a greater impact on the economic behavior of companies and individuals than statutory rates. Marginal effective rates reflect the net effect of special tax provisions on statutory rates. They are to be distinguished from average effective rates, which measure someone's tax burden.

Current statutory and effective individual tax rates are the result of the Tax Reform Act of 1986 (TRA86; P.L. 99-514) and several tax laws that have been enacted since 1986. Of particular importance are the Omnibus Budget Reconciliation Act of 1990 (OBRA90; P.L. 101-508), the Omnibus Budget Reconciliation Act of 1993 (OBRA93; P.L. 103-66), the Economic Growth and Tax Relief Reconciliation Act of 2001 (EGTRRA; P.L. 107-16), the Tax Relief, Unemployment Insurance Reauthorization, and Job Creation Act of 2010 (TRUC; P.L. 111-312), and the American Taxpayer Relief Act of 2012 (ATRA, P.L. 112-240). TRA86 made major changes in the income tax rate structure. EGTRRA established what are referred to as the Bush-era tax cuts for individuals. TRUC extended those cuts for another two years, through 2012. And ATRA permanently extended the Bush-era tax rates for taxpayers with taxable incomes below $400,000 for single filers and $450,000 for joint filers but reinstated the 39.6% top rate established by OBRA93 for taxpayers with taxable incomes equal to or above those amounts.

There are seven statutory individual income tax rates in 2013 for ordinary income: 10%, 15%, 25%, 28%, 33%, 35%, and 39.6%. Income from long-term capital gains and dividends is taxed at 0% for individuals subject to the 15% tax bracket; 15% for individuals subject to the 25%, 28%, 33%, or 35% brackets; and 20% for taxpayers taxed at 39.6%. Starting in 2013, a 3.8% tax is imposed on the lesser of net investment income received by individuals, estates, or trusts, or the amount of their modified adjusted gross incomes above the threshold amounts of $250,000 for joint filers and $125,000 for single filers. In addition, the individual alternative minimum tax (AMT), which functions like a separate income tax in that its rate structure is more compressed and tax base wider than those of the regular income tax, taxes income above exemption amounts of $80,800 for joint filers and $51,900 for single filers in 2013 at rates of 26% and 28%.

Tax rates and the income brackets to which they apply are not the only elements of the individual income tax that determine the tax liabilities of taxpayers. Personal exemptions, exclusions, deductions, credits, and certain other elements have an effect as well.

Some of these elements are indexed for inflation. Congress added annual indexation to the individual income tax in 1981. The primary advantage of such a mechanism is that it helps prevent real tax increases and unintended shifts in the distribution of the tax burden driven by inflation alone. Indexed elements include tax rate brackets, personal exemptions and their phaseout thresholds, standard deductions, the itemized deduction limitation threshold, and the AMT exemption amounts.

This report summarizes the tax brackets and other key elements of the individual income tax that help determine taxpayers' marginal and average effective tax rates going back to 1988. It is updated annually to reflect the most recent indexation adjustments and any statutory changes.

Contents

Tables

Contacts

Three Commonly Used Concepts of Tax Rates and How They Differ

In discussing U.S. individual income tax rates, one should be clear about which rates are being discussed. Three common measures of the tax rates people pay on their income are statutory rates, marginal effective rates, and average effective rates. Each has its own meaning. Those interested in how income taxes affect the economic behavior of households would benefit from having a clear understanding of the ways in which the three rates differ and the implications of these differences for the economic analysis of income taxes.

Statutory individual income tax rates (STRs) are the rates prescribed by law that apply to specified tiers or brackets of taxable income. The applicable rate depends on the size of a person's taxable income. Since the federal income tax is progressive in nature, taxpayers with relatively low taxable incomes face lower STRs than do taxpayers with relatively high taxable incomes.

Marginal effective tax rates (MERs) indicate the percentage of an additional dollar of income that is paid in taxes. This means that the rates take into account any tax provisions (e.g., special deductions or exemptions) that modify the applicable statutory rates.

By contrast, a taxpayer's average effective rate (AER) is her income tax liability divided by some measure of her total income. The tax liability is assumed to incorporate any special tax provisions that modified her taxable income or taxes paid in a tax year.

MERs, AERs, and STRs may differ considerably for some taxpayers. According to a 2005 report by the Congressional Budget Office (CBO) on marginal effective tax rates for labor income, a married couple with two children and a gross income in 2005 of between $14,370 and $35,263 faced an STR of 10% but an MER of 31.06%, owing to the phaseout of the earned income tax credit (EITC).[1] But in many cases, the STRs and MERs are the same or nearly so. In the same report, CBO found that most taxpayers faced MERs of 15% or less; less than 20% faced rates above 25%; and about 7% faced rates above 30%.[2] Still, for many individuals, the interaction between special provisions in the tax code and their personal circumstances leads to differences between their effective and statutory rates. Among the provisions that can drive a wedge between the two rates are the EITC,[3] the alternative minimum tax (AMT),[4] and personal exemptions and deductions.[5] Personal circumstances that can cause MERs to diverge from STRs include the sources of a taxpayer's income, itemized deductions, the number of children (if any) eligible for the child tax credit and EITC, and filing status.[6]

---

[1] See U.S. Congressional Budget Office, *Effective Marginal Tax Rates on Labor Income,* November 2005, p. 2; available at http://cbo.gov/ftpdocs/68xx/doc6854/11-10-LaborTaxation.pdf.

[2] Ibid., p. 1.

[3] For more information see CRS Report RL31768, *The Earned Income Tax Credit (EITC): An Overview*, by Christine Scott.

[4] For more information see CRS Report RL30149, *The Alternative Minimum Tax for Individuals*, by Steven Maguire.

[5] For more details see CRS Report R40508, *Personal Exemption Phaseout (PEP) and Limitation on Itemized Deductions (Pease)*, by Gary Guenther.

[6] Congressional Budget Office, *Effective Marginal Tax Rates on Labor Income*, p. 3.

Most economists believe that taxpayers change their economic behavior in response to MERs, not to statutory rates. Drawing on their standard model of consumer behavior, they argue that a person's MER influences many different decisions concerning whether and how much to work, how much to spend, and how much to save. For example, someone's MER may help determine whether he takes on an overtime shift, bargains for wages and benefits, takes a second job, or even enters the labor force. The idea that MERs affect an individual's economic behavior can be extended beyond the individual income tax to encompass an entire tax system, such as federal payroll and excise taxes, as well as state and local taxes.[7] A broader analysis along these lines, however, is, beyond the scope of this report.

Major Legislation Affecting Statutory Rates Since 1986

The current income tax is a product of the Tax Reform Act of 1986 (TRA86; P.L. 99-514). Among other things, the act reduced the individual tax rate structure to two statutory rates: 15% and 28%. TRA86 also included a 5% surcharge on the taxable income of certain upper-income households, effectively adding a third marginal tax rate of 33%.

In the 27 or so years since the enactment of TRA86, several other major changes in the federal individual income tax rate structure have been made. The Omnibus Budget Reconciliation Act of 1990 (OBRA90; P.L. 101-508) eliminated the 5% surcharge and replaced it with a statutory rate of 31%. In addition, OBRA90 imposed a limit on the amount of itemized deductions upper-income households could claim and accelerated the phaseout of personal exemptions for upper-income households. These provisions had the effect of raising effective tax rates above statutory tax rates for affected taxpayers.

The Omnibus Budget Reconciliation Act of 1993 (OBRA93; P.L. 103-66) added two new statutory rates (36% and 39.6%) at the upper end of the income scale. It also delayed indexation of the two new tax brackets for one year and permanently extended the limitation on itemized deductions and the accelerated phaseout of the personal exemption from OBRA90.

The Economic Growth and Tax Relief Reconciliation Act of 2001 (EGTRRA; P.L. 107-16) created a new 10% statutory rate. It also included a phased-in reduction in the top four statutory rates to 25%, 28%, 33%, and 35%. Several other provisions of the act modified tax brackets and limitations on personal exemptions and deductions for higher income taxpayers. The Jobs and Growth Tax Relief Reconciliation Act of 2003 (JGTRRA; P.L. 108-27), Working Families Tax Relief Act of 2004 (WFTRA; P.L. 108-311), and the Tax Increase Prevention and Reconciliation Act of 2005 (TIPRA; P.L. 109-222) collectively accelerated and extended the tax rate reductions originally enacted under EGTRRA through 2010.[8] Under a last-minute agreement reached between President Obama and congressional leaders from both parties, Congress passed a measure (the Tax Relief, Unemployment Insurance Reauthorization, and Job Creation Act of

---

[7] For an example of such analysis, see S. D. Holt and J. L. Romich, (2007), "Marginal Tax Rates Facing Low- and Moderate-Income Workers Who Participate in Means-Tested Transfer Programs," *National Tax Journal*, vol. 60, no. 2, June 2007, p. 253.

[8] For more details see CRS Report R41111, *Expiration and Extension of the Individual Income Tax Cuts First Enacted in 2001 and 2003: Background and Analysis*, by James M. Bickley.

2010, TRUC, P.L. 111-312) that extended the Bush-era individual income tax cuts through 2012. Facing the unwanted prospect of an across-the-board increase in all STRs, the 112ᵗʰ Congress passed a measure (American Taxpayer Relief Act of 2012 (ATRA, P.L. 112-240) permanently extending each of the Bush-era STRs with one exception: the top rate increased from 35% to 39.6%. Each of these major acts is described in more detail below.

Tax Reform Act of 1986

Among its many changes, TRA86 simplified the individual income tax rate structure for tax years after 1987 by replacing the 14 non-zero statutory rates that applied to the 1985 and 1986 tax years with two such rates: 15% and 28%. **Table 3** shows the key elements of the 1988 tax rate structure. These rates applied to capital income as well as to labor income.

Although TRA86 established only two statutory individual marginal income tax rates, it also adopted a 5% surcharge on the taxable income of certain upper-income households. This surcharge effectively created a third statutory tax rate of 33% (a 28% statutory tax rate plus a 5% surcharge).

Because the surcharge phased in over a certain range of income and then phased out as incomes increased, statutory tax rates rose to 33% but then fell back to 28%, producing what was known as the tax rate "bubble." The intent of the surcharge was two-fold: (1) to prevent TRA86 from changing the distribution of the income tax burden among income groups relative to its distribution under pre-1986 tax law, and (2) to meet specified revenue targets.

More specifically, the surcharge was designed to eliminate the tax benefits of both the 15% tax bracket and the personal exemptions for upper-income households. For joint returns in 1988, the phaseout of the 15% tax rate started when taxable income exceeded $71,900 and ended when taxable income reached $149,250; the phaseout of the exemptions followed from that point on. For single returns, the phaseout of the 15% tax bracket occurred when taxable income was between $47,050 and $97,620. For heads of households, the phaseout occurred when taxable income fell in the range of $67,200 to $134,930. The phaseout of the exemptions followed the phaseout of the 15% tax bracket for all filers, but the range of income over which it took place depended on the number of exemptions claimed by a taxpayer.

To demonstrate how the 5% surcharge worked to "phase out" the tax benefits of the 15% tax bracket consider the following example based on joint returns for 1988. The difference between taxing the first $29,750 of taxable income at 28% instead of 15% was $3,867.50 (obtained as $29,750 multiplied by 13%, the difference between 28% and 15%). Five percent of the difference between the upper and lower phaseout limits also equaled $3,867.50 ($149,250 less $71,900 multiplied by 5%). Hence, assessing the 5% surcharge on taxable income between $78,400 and $162,770 was equivalent to taxing the first $32,450 of taxable income at 28% rather than 15%.

A 5% surcharge was also used to phase out the tax benefit from the personal exemption for upper-income households. In 1988, each personal exemption was worth $1,950 and produced a tax savings for a household in the 28% tax rate bracket of $546 ($1,950 times 28%). To recapture these tax savings, a 5% surcharge was assessed against $10,920 of taxable income for each personal exemption claimed. The result was an increase in tax liability of $546 ($10,920 times 5%), the same amount as the tax savings from the personal exemption.

The phaseout of personal exemptions started immediately after the phaseout of the 15% tax bracket and occurred sequentially for each exemption. This meant that the taxable income range over which the 5% surcharge offset personal exemptions depended on the number of personal exemptions claimed on the tax return. For example, on a joint return claiming two personal exemptions, the 5% surcharge would apply to taxable income between $149,250 and $171,090 ($149,250 plus two times $10,920). On a joint return with four personal exemptions, the 5% surcharge would apply to taxable income between $149,250 and $192,930 ($149,250 plus four times $10,920).

Omnibus Budget Reconciliation Act of 1990

The Omnibus Budget Reconciliation Act of 1990 (OBRA90) created a three-tiered statutory marginal income tax rate structure with rates of 15%, 28%, and 31%, effective in tax years beginning in 1991, as shown in **Table 5**. OBRA90 eliminated the tax bubble created under TRA86, but replaced it with a limitation on itemized deductions and a new approach to phasing out the tax benefits of the personal exemption for upper-income households.

OBRA90 reintroduced a tax-rate differential on capital gains income. OBRA90 contained a provision which limited the tax on capital gains income to a maximum of 28%. This provision was effective starting in tax year 1991. Under TRA86, capital gains had been treated as ordinary income and taxed at regular rates of up to 33%.

The OBRA90 limitation on itemized deductions worked as follows. For tax years starting in 1991, otherwise allowable deductions were reduced by 3% of the amount by which a taxpayer's adjusted gross income (AGI) exceeded $100,000 (or $50,000 in the case of married couples filing separate returns). For example, in 1991, if a taxpayer's AGI was $110,000, then his otherwise allowable itemized deductions would be reduced by $300 ($110,000 less $100,000 times 3%). This provision effectively raised the marginal income tax rate of those taxpayers affected by approximately one percentage point. A dollar of income in excess of $100,000 was taxed as if it were $1.03, since in addition to the tax on an extra dollar of income, the taxpayer lost tax deductions by giving up $0.03 of itemized deductions.

This limitation was scheduled to expire after tax year 1995 under OBRA90, but was later extended. Allowable deductions for medical expenses, casualty and theft losses, and investment interest were not subject to this limitation. For tax years after 1991, the $100,000 threshold was indexed for inflation.

The phaseout of the tax benefits of the personal exemption worked as follows. Each personal exemption was phased out by a factor of 2% for each $2,500 (or fraction thereof) by which a taxpayer's AGI exceeded a given threshold amount. In 1991, the threshold amount for a joint return was $150,000; for a single return the threshold was $100,000; and for heads of households the threshold was $125,000.

For example, in 1991, a joint household whose AGI was $183,000 would lose 28% of their total personal exemptions claimed. The AGI amount in excess of the threshold in this instance would be $33,000, $183,000 AGI less $150,000 threshold limit. The $33,000 excess divided by $2,500 would produce a factor of 13.2, which when rounded up would equal 14. This figure is multiplied by 2% to arrive at the final disallowance amount of 28%. Hence, if the family had claimed two personal exemptions, which at $2,150 each would total $4,300, they would only be allowed to deduct $3,096 ($4,300 total personal exemptions less the $1,204 disallowance, which is 28% of the total).

For tax years after 1991, these income threshold amounts were indexed for inflation. The personal exemptions phaseout provision was also scheduled to expire after tax year 1995.

Omnibus Budget Reconciliation Act of 1993

The Omnibus Budget Reconciliation Act of 1993 (OBRA93) made several changes in the individual marginal income tax rate structure. First, it added two new marginal tax rates, 36% and 39.6%, at the upper end of the income spectrum. The 39.6% tax bracket was the result of adding a 10% surtax to the 36% rate for taxpayers with taxable incomes over $250,000 in 1993.

Although OBRA93 was enacted in August of 1993, the increase in the top marginal tax rates was made effective retroactively to January 1, 1993. Affected taxpayers, however, were not assessed penalties for underpayment of 1993 taxes resulting from the tax rate increase. Taxpayers were also allowed to pay any additional 1993 taxes in three equal installments over a two-year period.

Second, OBRA93 delayed indexation of the new top marginal income tax brackets for one year. Hence, the nominal dollar tax brackets for the 36% and 39.6% marginal tax rates remained at the same level for both tax years 1993 and 1994.

Finally, OBRA93 made permanent both the itemized deduction limitation and the phaseout of the tax benefits from personal exemptions.

Economic Growth and Tax Relief Reconciliation Act of 2001

The Economic Growth and Tax Relief Reconciliation Act of 2001 (EGTRRA) made several major changes to the marginal tax rate structure. Many of the act's provisions were set to phase in over a period of time, but subsequent legislation, described in the next section, overrode the schedule originally set by EGTRRA. **Table 1** shows the time line of changes related to the marginal tax rate structure enacted under EGTRRA and the subsequent bills. All of the EGTRRA provisions, as amended, expire at the end of 2010.

First, the 2001 act created a new 10% bracket. It applied, beginning in tax year 2002, to the first $12,000 of taxable income for married couples filing jointly, the first $10,000 of taxable income for heads of households, and the first $6,000 of taxable income for single individuals. For tax year 2001, the act created a "rate reduction tax credit," mimicking the effects of the 10% tax rate bracket for most taxpayers.[9]

EGTRRA gradually phased in and expanded the bracket over several years, but in 2003-2007, these provisions of EGTRRA were accelerated by subsequent legislation. In 2008, EGTRRA became effective again, setting the 10% marginal tax rate bracket at $7,000 and $14,000 for single and married taxpayers, respectively. Starting with tax year 2009, these bracket amounts are indexed for inflation.

---

[9] For more information see CRS Report RS21171, *The Rate Reduction Tax Credit - "The Tax Rebate" - in the Economic Growth and Tax Relief Reconciliation Act of 2001: A Brief Explanation*, by Steven Maguire.

Second, the 2001 act gradually reduced the top four marginal income tax rates. Under prior income tax law, the top four marginal tax rates were 28%, 31%, 36%, and 39.6%. When fully phased in, the 2001 act reduced the top four marginal income tax rates to 25%, 28%, 33%, and 35%. Once again, under EGTRRA the reductions were scheduled to take place in 2001 through 2006, but subsequent legislation accelerated the EGTRRA phase-in schedule.

Third, EGTRRA also repealed the limitation on itemized deductions and personal exemptions for high-income taxpayers. The repeal was phased in between 2006 and 2009. The limitation is completely repealed for 2010, but it would reappear again in 2011, once the EGTRRA's tax cuts expire.

Fourth, some of the act's measures designed to reduce the marriage penalty affected the rate bracket structure. The act increased the width of the 15% tax bracket for married couples filing joint returns to twice the width of the 15% tax bracket for single returns. Under EGTRRA this provision was scheduled for phase-in over a four-year time period starting in 2005, but subsequent legislation accelerated this time line. Under EGTRRA, the end point of the 15% tax bracket for joint returns was scheduled to be 180% of the end point of the 15% tax bracket for single returns in 2005, 187% in 2006, 193% in 2007, and 200% in 2008 and subsequent years.[10]

Finally, the 2001 act increased the standard deduction for joint returns to twice the size of the standard deduction for single returns. The change was scheduled to be phased in over a five-year period, 2005 to 2009, but it was accelerated by the subsequent bills as well. This had an effect, as far as tax rate brackets were concerned, of raising the lower threshold of the lowest tax bracket for married taxpayers.

Jobs and Growth Tax Relief Reconciliation Act of 2003 and Subsequent Legislation

Among the several acts extending provisions of EGTRRA, the following directly affected statutory income tax rates: the Jobs and Growth Tax Relief Reconciliation Act of 2003 (JGTRRA), the Working Families Tax Relief Act of 2004 (WFTRA), the Tax Increase Prevention and Reconciliation Act of 2005 (TIPRA), the Tax Relief, Unemployment Insurance Reauthorization, and Job Creation Act of 2010 (TRUC), and the American Taxpayer Relief Act of 2012.

JGTRRA accelerated several changes to the individual income tax rate structure first enacted under EGTRRA. It moved forward to 2003 the tax rate reductions, the expansion of the 10% tax bracket, and the widening of the 15% tax bracket for joint returns to make it double the width of the 15% tax bracket for single returns. Under EGTRRA, some of these changes would not have been fully phased in until 2009.

WFTRA extended several tax provisions of JGTRRA that were scheduled to expire at the end of 2004. Among other things, it extended the increase in the 10% income tax bracket through 2007, at which point EGTRRA's relevant provisions were fully phased in, maintaining a constant level of the tax relief.

---

[10] For more information on these changes see CRS Report R41111, *Expiration and Extension of the Individual Income Tax Cuts First Enacted in 2001 and 2003: Background and Analysis*, by James M. Bickley.

WFTRA also extended marriage penalty relief through 2008. The standard deduction and 15% tax bracket for joint returns were set at twice their level for single returns. In 2009 and 2010, EGTRRA provisions applied, maintaining the same level of tax relief.

JGTRRA also established a more preferential tax rates for long-term capital gains and dividends. It reduced the rates applicable to these kinds of income to 15%, and even 0% for certain low-income taxpayers. These changes were set to expire at the end of 2008, but TIPRA extended them through the end of 2010.

A last-minute agreement in 2010 between President Obama and congressional leaders of both parties cleared the way for an extension of all the Bush-era individual tax cuts through the end of 2012. TRUC was the legislative vehicle for the extension.

Under the threat of a return of each statutory tax rate to its level before the enactment of EGTRRA starting January 1, 2013, Congress and President Obama agreed on legislation (ATRA) to extend permanently each of the Bush-era rates and raise the top marginal tax rate to its pre-EGTTRA level of 039.6%. The act also permanently extends the repeal of the phaseout of the personal exemption included in EGTRRA, but it restricts the phaseout to taxpayers with AGIs of $250,000 or less for single filers and $300,000 or less for married couples filing jointly. Taxpayers with AGIs above these inflation-adjusted amounts are subject to the phaseout. The same rule applies to the repeal under EGTRRA of the so-called Pease limitation on the amount of itemized deductions an upper-income taxpayer could take.

Table 1. Phase-in and Expiration of Select Provisions Under EGTRRA and Subsequent Legislation

Provision	2001	2002	2003	2004	2005	2006	2007	2008	2009	2010	2011	2012	2013
Tax Rates and Brackets													
Create 10% tax bracket	EGTRRA: $12,000 / $6,000 brackets for couples / singles.		JGTRRA: $14,000 / $7,000 for couples / singles. Index in 2004.		WFTRA: $14,000 / $7,000 for couples / singles.			EGTRRA: $14,000 / $7,000 for couples / singles. Index in 2009.			TRUC extended the bracket through 2012.		ATRA: Permanently extended the bracket.
	EGTRRA:	EGTRRA:	JGTRRA:		JGTRRA:			EGTRRA:	EGTRRA:		TRUC:		ATRA: Permanently extended these brackets.
Reduce tax rates in top four tax brackets	39.1%	38.6%		35%				35%			35%		39.6%
	35.5%	35%		33%				33%			33%		35%
	30.5%	30%		28%				28%			28%		33%
	27.5%	27%		25%				25%			25%		28%
													25%
													ATRA: 0% for taxpayers in 10% bracket; 15% for taxpayers in 25% to 35% brackets; and 20% for taxpayers in 39.6% bracket.
Reduce tax rates on capital gains and dividends	No change.		JGTRRA: 15% or 5% rate depending on income.					JGTRRA: 15% / 0%	TIPRA: 15% / 0%	JGTRRA: 15% / 0%	TRUC: 15%/0		
Limits on Itemized Deductions and Personal Exemptions													
Reduce or eliminate limits on	No change.							EGTRRA:	EGTRRA:	EGTRRA:	TRUC:		ATRA:

CRS-8

Statutory Individual Income Tax Rates and Other Elements of the Tax System: 1988 throu

Provision	2001	2002	2003	2004	2005	2006	2007	2008	2009	2010	2011	2012	2013
itemized deductions and personal exemptions						Reduce limits by one-third.		Reduce limits by two-thirds.		Repeal limits.	Extended repeal until 2012.		Limits permanently reinstated for taxpayers with incomes above $250,000 for single filers and $300,000 for joint filers.

Marriage Penalty Relief

Provision	2001	2002	2003	2004	2005	2006	2007	2008	2009	2010	2011	2012	2013
Increase standard deduction for married couples	No change.		JGTRRA: Deduction for couples is 200% of the deduction for singles.			WFTRA: Deduction for couples is 200% of the deduction for singles.			EGTRRA: Deduction for couples is 200% of the deduction for singles.		TRUC: Extended the EGTRRA deduction through 2012.		ATRA: Permanently extended JGTRRA relief.
Expand 15% bracket for married couples	No change.		JGTRRA: Top of the bracket for couples is 200% of that for singles.			WFTRA: Top of the bracket for couples is 200% of that for singles.			EGTRRA: Top of the bracket for couples is 200% of that for singles.		TRUC: Extended the expanded 15% bracket for couples through 2012.		ATRA: Permanently extended JGTRRA relief.

Source: CRS adaptation of Congressional Budget Office and Joint Committee on Taxation tables and publications.

Note: EGTRRA—Economic Growth and Tax Relief Reconciliation Act of 2001 (P.L. 107-16, 2001, introduced as H.R. 1836); JGTRRA—Jobs and Growth Tax Relief Reconciliation Act of 2003 (P.L. 108-27, 2003, introduced as H.R. 2); WFTRA—Working Families Tax Relief Act of 2004 (P.L. 108-311, 2004, introduced as H.R. 1308); TIPRA—Tax Increase Prevention and Reconciliation Act of 2005 (P.L. 109-222, 2006, introduced as H.R. 4297); and ATRA—American Taxpayer Relief Act of 2012 (P.L. 112-240, 2012, introduced as H.R. 8).

Effects of Inflation on Income Tax Liabilities

During periods of inflation, a progressive income tax structure based on tax brackets set in nominal dollars can lead to automatic tax increases and unintended changes in the income distribution of the tax burden. This is because nominal incomes rise faster than real incomes, all other things being equal. As a result, tax burdens for taxpayers become larger than what lawmakers intended when they passed the laws setting existing statutory tax rates. In the absence of periodic indexation of the key elements of the tax code determining the tax burdens of individuals, a greater share of taxpayers will face growing tax liabilities because their nominal incomes will increase, irrespective of what happens to their real incomes.

The effects of inflation on income tax liabilities can be substantial, even in periods of low inflation, such as the last two decades or so. Still, according to the Bureau of Labor Statistics, $1,000 in 1988 is worth about $1,941 in 2012.[11] Year-to-year changes might appear negligible, but over a decade or so, those annual changes can add up to make a substantial difference through the power of compounding.

A hypothetical example can illustrate the implications over time of a lack of indexation for the tax burdens of individual taxpayers. Assume that the tax structure from 1988 applied without indexation or any other changes in 2012. Also assume that a family of four had an adjusted gross income (AGI) of $35,000 in 1988. If the family took the standard deduction, then its taxable income would have been $22,200 ($35,000 minus the standard deduction of $5,000 and four personal exemptions at $1,950 apiece), and its tax liability—$3,330. This translates into an after-tax income of $31,670 ($35,000 less $3,330), or an average tax rate of 9.5% ($3,270 divided by $35,000 income).

Now consider what would have happened to the family's tax burden in 2012 if the same family's nominal income had kept up with inflation but the 1988 tax structure had remained intact, with no indexation for inflation. The family's AGI would have been $67,929: $35,000 x 1.94 rise in the general price level as measured by the Consumer Price Index for all Urban Consumers. Its taxable income would have been $55,129, and its tax liability would have increased to $11,569 in 2012 dollars, or $5,961 in 1988 dollars ($11,569 adjusted for cumulative inflation of about 49%). This would have represented a 79% increase in the family's real tax liability (measured in 1988 dollars). The family's after-tax income would have been $56,360 in 2012 dollars, or $29,025 in 1988 dollars ($56,360 adjusted for a cumulative rise in the cost of living of about 49%), or a decrease of over 8% from 1988. Its average tax rate would have increased from 9.5 % to 17.0%.

So in the absence of the indexation, the family's real after-tax income would have declined by 8%, and its real income tax burden would have risen by 79% from 1988 to 2012. This striking discrepancy exemplifies what is known as "bracket creep." Such an effect would be even more pronounced during periods of high inflation.

Under an indexed income tax, the family would have experienced no change in their real after-tax income. With indexation, the value of the standard deduction for a joint return would have increased from $5,000 in 1988 to $9,700 in 2012, and the personal exemption for each family

[11] BLS, *CPI Inflation Calculator,* website, at http://www.bls.gov/data/inflation_calculator.htm/.

member would have increased from $1,950 to $3,783. Under these circumstances, the family's 2012 taxable income would have been $43,079 ($67,929 income less standard deduction and personal exemptions). Tax brackets would have adjusted as well. Based on this taxable income and the adjusted brackets, their income tax liability would have been $6,465, or $3,329 in 1988 dollars—about the same as it was in 1988 (the difference is due to rounding). In short, the nominal amounts would have risen, but the real values would have stayed the same for this family.

Congress added indexation to the individual income tax as a part of the overall package of statutory tax rate reductions contained in the Economic Recovery Tax Act of 1981. The U.S. rate of inflation was unusually high at the time.

> The Congress believed that "automatic" tax increases resulting from the effects of inflation were unfair to taxpayers, since their tax burden as a percentage of income could increase during intervals between tax reduction legislation, with an adverse effect on incentives to work and invest. In addition, the Federal Government was provided with an automatic increase in its aggregate revenue, which in turn created pressure for further spending.[12]

Since 1981, the list of indexed elements has gradually expanded and now consists of more than three dozen tax parameters. One notable expansion occurred with TRA86, which extended indexation to some newly created elements of the tax code, including the standard deductions for the elderly and the blind and the EITC. More recently, EGTRRA indexed the phaseout amounts for the EITC, starting in 2008.

Table 2 lists the major indexed tax items and provides the first year of for the adjustment.[13]

Table 2. Indexed Elements of the Individual Income Tax System

Item	Base Period Is the 12-Month Period Ending	Adjustment First Occurs in Calendar Year
Standard deduction	31-Aug-87	1989
Unearned income of minor child (base amount)	31-Aug-87	1989
Exemptions	31-Aug-88	1990
Educational savings bonds	31-Aug-89	1991
Exemption phaseout	31-Aug-90	1992
Itemized deduction limitation (3% of AGI)	31-Aug-90	1992
Tax rate schedules:		
10% bracket	31-Aug-02	2004
15%, 25%, 28% brackets	31-Aug-92	1994
33%, 35%, 39.6% brackets	31-Aug-93	1995

---

[12] U.S. Congress, Joint Committee on Taxation, *General Explanation of the Economic Recovery Tax Act of 1981,* JCS-71-81, December 31, 1981, as redistributed by CCH Internet Tax Research NetWork.

[13] James C. Young, "A Summary of 2007 Inflation Adjustments Impacting Individuals," *Tax Notes,* Oct. 15, 2007, p. 246.

Item	Base Period Is the 12-Month Period Ending	Adjustment First Occurs in Calendar Year
Alternative minimum tax:		
Exemption amounts for single and joint filers	31-Aug-13	2014
Earned income credit:		
Base amounts and maximum earned income amount	31-Aug-95	1997
Married phaseout base	31-Aug-08	2010
Standard deduction for employed dependents	31-Aug-97	1999
Medical savings accounts	31-Aug-97	1999
Annual gift tax exclusion	31-Aug-97	1999
Qualified transportation fringe benefits:		
Categories 1 and 2	31-Aug-01	2003
Category 3	31-Aug-98	2000
HOPE, lifetime learning, and child tax credits	31-Aug-00	2002
Education loan interest	31-Aug-01	2003
Adoption expenses/credit		
Credit/exclusion amount	31-Aug-09	2011
Phaseout base	31-Aug-01	2003
Traditional and Roth IRAs		
Income phaseout	31-Aug-05	2007
Contribution Limit	31-Aug-07	2009
Section 179 expense amounts	31-Aug-06	2008

Source: James C. Young, "Inflation Adjustments Affecting Individual Taxpayers in 2012," *Tax Notes*, Dec. 5, 2011

Indexing may compound the complexity of the individual income tax, but given its benefits to taxpayers over time, this is a minor matter. The year-to-year changes in dollar amounts are usually small, so taxpayers seldom, if ever, face unexpected changes that might materially affect them. On the revenue side, indexing results in lower government receipts.

But some key elements of the tax remain unadjusted for inflation, giving rise to significant policy challenges from time to time. One such element is the child tax credit. Under current law, the amount of the credit itself and the phaseout thresholds for higher-income taxpayers are not adjusted for inflation. But the earned income floor used in calculating the credit's refundable amount is adjusted for inflation.[14] Consequently, inflation would erode the value of the credit and reduce the number of eligible taxpayers at both ends of the income spectrum in the long run under

---

[14] In 2008-2010 the amount of the threshold was set by special provisions of the Emergency Economic Stabilization Act of 2008 (P.L. 110-343) and the American Recovery and Reinvestment Act of 2009 (P.L. 111-5), but these provisions are currently set to expire at the end of 2010.

current law. Another element not indexed for inflation is the threshold amounts for determining who pays the 3.8% tax on net investment income that takes effect in 2013.

The Mechanics of Indexation

Most elements are indexed using the technical calculation described below. In some instances, the calculation methodology differs somewhat in one way or another. Examples include the EITC or transportation benefits. The variations are insignificant, as long as they do not result in systematic deviations from the rate of inflation.

The adjustment for any given tax year is based on the percentage amount by which the average Consumer Price Index for all items for all urban consumers (CPI-U) for the 12-month period ending on August 31 of the preceding year exceeds the average CPI-U during a 12-month base period. Not all indexed tax elements use the same base period, as shown in **Table 2**.

With the exception of the EITC, inflation adjustments are rounded down to the nearest multiple of $50. Although rounding down affects the accuracy of any given year's inflation adjustment, the effect is not cumulative since each year's adjustment reflects the entire amount of inflation that has occurred between the adjustment year and the base period.

For example, the adjustment factor for the personal exemption in 2012 was calculated as follows. By law, the base period for this factor is September 1987 through August 1988, when the average CPI-U was 116.6. The average CPI-U for the period September 2010 through August 2011, on which the 2012 value is based, was 222.4. Thus, the inflation adjustment factor in 2012 was 1.91 (222.4/116.6). This factor was then applied to $2,000, the value of the exemption in 1989, resulting in $3,820. Rounding this number down to the nearest multiple of $50 yielded the final value of the exemption in 2012: $3,800.

Since the onset of the Great Recession in late 2007, the U.S. inflation rate has fluctuated between -0.4% and 3.2%, as measured by the CPI-U on a year-to-year basis. Negative inflation, or deflation, occurred in 2009 relative to 2008. Deflation denotes a decrease in the general price level. As a result, the inflation adjustments in 2010 were either very small or non-existent. Several other federal programs experienced similar situations, even though they do not use the same indexing methodology. For example, there was no cost-of-living adjustment for Social Security benefits in 2010.[15]

If the United States were to experience a sustained deflation, the income tax elements could be reduced in real dollars. By law, however, the elements cannot fall below their base-year values. Since their current values are much higher than their base values, which were established years ago, it is unlikely this limitation will come into play anytime soon for most indexed elements.

---

[15] For more information please see CRS Report R40561, *Interactions Between the Social Security COLA and Medicare Part B Premiums*, by Jim Hahn.

Tax Rate Schedules for 1988 Through 2013

The following tables present the personal exemption amounts, standard deductions, and the statutory marginal tax rates schedules for each tax year from 1988 through 2013.

Table 3. Personal Exemptions, Standard Deductions, and Statutory Tax Rates, 1988

Personal Exemptions	$1,950

Standard Deductions	
Joint	$5,000
Single	$3,000
Head of Household	$4,400

Additional Standard Deduction for the Elderly or the Blind	
Joint	$600
Single/Head of Household	$750

Statutory Marginal Income Tax Rates, Joint Returns	
If *taxable income* is:	Then, *tax* is:
$0 to $29,750	15% of the amount over $0
over $29,750 to $71,900	$4,462.50 + 28% of the amount over $29,750
over $71,900 to $171,090[a]	$16,264.50 + 33% of the amount over $71,900
over $171,090	$47,905.20 + 28% of the amount over $171,090

Statutory Marginal Income Tax Rates, Single Returns	
If *taxable income* is:	Then, *tax* is:
$0 to $17,850	15% of the amount over $0
over $17,850 to $43,150	$2,677.50 + 28% of the amount over $17,850
over $43,150 to $100,480[a]	$9,761.50 + 33% of the amount over $43,150
over $100,480	$28,134.40 + 28% of the amount over $100,480

Statutory Marginal Income Tax Rates, Head-of-Household Returns	
If *taxable income* is:	Then, *tax* is:
$0 to $23,900	15% of the amount over $0
over $23,900 to $61,650	$3,585 + 28% of the amount over $23,900
over $61,650 to $145,630[a]	$14,155 + 33% of the amount over $61,650
over $145,630	$40,776.40 + 28% of the amount over $145,630

a. Implicit tax bracket, generated by the "tax bubble," as described in text. The bracket's upper bound depends on the number of exemptions claimed by the taxpayer. The example in this table assumes one exemption for single returns, two for the other statuses.

Table 4. Personal Exemptions, Standard Deductions, and Statutory Tax Rates, 1989

Personal Exemptions	$2,000

Standard Deductions	

Joint	$5,200
Single	$3,100
Head of Household	$4,550

Additional Standard Deduction for the Elderly or the Blind	
Joint	$600
Single/Head of Household	$750

Statutory Marginal Income Tax Rates, Joint Returns	
If *taxable income* is:	Then, *tax* is:
$0 to $30,950	15% of the amount over $0
over $30,950 to $ 74,850	$4,642.50 + 28% of the amount over $30,950
over $ 74,850 to $177,720[a]	$16,934.50 + 33% of the amount over $74,850
over $177,720	$50,881.60 + 28% of the amount over $177,720

Statutory Marginal Income Tax Rates, Single Returns	
If *taxable income* is:	Then, *tax* is:
$0 to $18,550	15% of the amount over $0
over $18,550 to $ 44,900	$2,782.50 + 28% of the amount over $18,550
over $44,900 to $104,300[a]	$10,160.50 + 33% of the amount over $44,900
over $104,300	$29,772.40 + 28% of the amount over $104,300

Statutory Marginal Income Tax Rates, Head-of-Household Returns	
If *taxable income* is:	Then, *tax* is:
$0 to $24,850	15% of the amount over $0
over $24,850 to $ 64,200	$ 3,727.50 + 28% of the amount over $ 24,850
over $64,200 to $151,210a	$14,745.50 + 33% of the amount over $ 64,200
over $151,210	$43,458.80 + 28% of the amount over $151,210

a.   Implicit tax bracket, generated by the "tax bubble," as described in text. The bracket's upper bound depends on the number of exemptions claimed by the taxpayer. The example in this table assumes one exemption for single returns, two for the other statuses.

Table 5. Personal Exemptions, Standard Deductions, and Statutory Tax Rates, 1990

Personal Exemptions	$2,050
Standard Deductions	
Joint	$5,450
Single	$3,250
Head of Household	$4,750

Additional Standard Deductions for the Elderly or the Blind	
Joint	$650
Single/Head of Household	$800

Statutory Marginal Income Tax Rates, Joint Returns	
If *taxable income* is:	Then, *tax* is:

$0 to $32,450	15% of the amount over $0
over $32,450 to $78,400	$,867.50 + 28% of the amount over $32,450
over $78,400 to $185,730ª	$17,733.50 + 33% of the amount over $78,400
over $185,730	$53,152.40 + 28% of the amount over $185,730

Statutory Marginal Income Tax Rates, Single Returns

If *taxable income* is:	Then, *tax* is:
$0 to $19,450	15% of the amount over $0
over $19,450 to $47,050	$2,917.50 + 28% of the amount over $19,450
over $47,050 to $109,100ª	$10,645.50 + 33% of the amount over $47,050
over $109,100	$31,122.00 + 28% of the amount over $109,100

Statutory Marginal Income Tax Rates, Head-of-Household Returns

If *taxable income* is:	Then, *tax* is:
$0 to $26,050	15% of the amount over $0
over $ 26,050 to $67,200	$3,907.50 + 28% of the amount over $26,050
over $67,200 to $157,890ª	$15,429.50 + 33% of the amount over $67,200
over $157,890	$45,357.20 + 28% of the amount over $157,890

a. Implicit tax bracket, generated by the "tax bubble," as described in text. The bracket's upper bound depends on the number of exemptions claimed by the taxpayer. The example in this table assumes one exemption for single returns, two for the other statuses.

Table 6. Personal Exemptions, Standard Deductions, and Statutory Tax Rates, 1991

Personal Exemptions	$2,150
Standard Deductions	
Joint	$5,700
Single	$3,400
Head of Household	$5,000
Additional Standard Deductions for the Elderly or the Blind	
Joint	$650
Single/Head of Household	$850

Statutory Marginal Income Tax Rates, Joint Returns

If *taxable income* is:	Then, *tax* is:
$0 to $34,000	15% of the amount over $0
over $34,000 to $82,150	$5,100 + 28% of the amount over $34,000
over $82,150	$18,582 + 31% of the amount over $82,150

Statutory Marginal Income Tax Rates, Single Returns

If *taxable income* is:	Then, *tax* is:
$0 to $20,350	15% of the amount over $0
over $20,350 to $49,300	$3,052.50 + 28% of the amount over $20,350
over $49,300	$11,158.50 + 31% of the amount over $ 49,300

Statutory Marginal Income Tax Rates, Head-of-Household Returns

If *taxable income* is:	Then, *tax* is:
$0 to $27,300	15% of the amount over $0
over $27,300 - $70,450	$4,095 + 28% of the amount over $27,300
over $70,450	$16,177 + 31% of the amount over $70,450

Table 7. Personal Exemptions, Standard Deductions, and Statutory Tax Rates, 1992

Personal Exemptions	$2,300
Standard Deductions	
Joint	$6,000
Single	$3,600
Head of Household	$5,250
Additional Standard Deductions for the Elderly or the Blind	
Joint	$700
Single/Head of Household	$900

Statutory Marginal Income Tax Rates, Joint Returns

If *taxable income* is:	Then, *tax* is:
$0 to $35,800	15% of the amount over $0
over $35,800 to $86,500	$5,370 + 28% of the amount over $35,800
over $86,500	$19,566 + 31% of the amount over $86,500

Statutory Marginal Income Tax Rates, Single Returns

If *taxable income* is:	Then, *tax* is:
$0 - $21,450	15% of the amount over $0
over $21,450 to $51,900	$3,218 + 28% of the amount over $21,450
over $51,900	$11,744 + 31% of the amount over $51,900

Statutory Marginal Income Tax Rates, Head-of-Household Returns

If *taxable income* is:	Then, *tax* is:
$0 - $28,750	15% of the amount over $0
over $28,750 to $ 74,150	$4,313 + 28% of the amount over $28,750
over $ 4,150	$17,235 + 31% of the amount over $74,150

Table 8. Personal Exemptions, Standard Deductions, and Statutory Tax Rates, 1993

Personal Exemptions	$2,350

Standard Deductions	
Joint	$6,200
Single	$3,700
Head of Household	$5,450

Additional Standard Deductions for the Elderly or the Blind	
Joint	$700
Single/Head of Household	$900

Statutory Marginal Income Tax Rates, Joint Returns

If *taxable income* is:	Then, *tax* is:
$0 to $36,900	15% of the amount over $0
over $36,900 to $89,150	$5,535 + 28% of the amount over $36,900
over $89,150 to $140,000	$20,165 + 31% of the amount over $89,150
over $140,000 to $250,000	$35,929 + 36% of the amount over $140,000
over $250,000	$75,529 + 39.6% of the amount over $250,000

Statutory Marginal Income Tax Rates, Single Returns

If *taxable income* is:	Then, *tax* is:
$0 to $22,100	15% of the amount over $0
over $22,100 to $53,500	$3,315 + 28% of the amount over $22,100
over $53,500 to $115,000	$12,107 + 31% of the amount over $53,500
over $115,000 to $250,000	$31,172 + 36% of the amount over $115,000
over $250,000	$79,772 + 39.6% of the amount over $250,000

Statutory Marginal Income Tax Rates, Head-of-Household Returns

If *taxable income* is:	Then, *tax* is:
$0 to $29,600	15% of the amount over $0
over $29,600 to $76,400	$4,440 + 28% of the amount over $29,600
over$76,400 to $127,500	$17,544 + 31% of the amount over $76,400
over $127,500 to $250,000	$33,385 + 36% of the amount over $127,500
over $250,000	$77,485 + 39.6% of the amount over $250,000

Table 9. Personal Exemptions, Standard Deductions, and Statutory Tax Rates, 1994

Personal Exemptions	$2,450

Standard Deductions	
Joint	$6,350
Single	$3,800
Head of Household	$5,600

Additional Standard Deductions for the Elderly or the Blind	
Joint	$750
Single/Head of Household	$950

Statutory Marginal Income Tax Rates, Joint Returns	
If *taxable income* is:	Then, *tax* is:
$0 to $38,000	15% of the amount over $0
over $38,000 to $91,850	$5,700 + 28% of the amount over $38,000
over $91,850 to $140,000	$20,778 + 31% of the amount over $91,850
over $140,000 to $250,000	$35,705 + 36% of the amount over $140,000
over $250,000	$75,305 + 39.6% of the amount over $250,000

Statutory Marginal Income Tax Rates, Single Returns	
If *taxable income* is:	Then, *tax* is:
$0 to $22,750	15% of the amount over $0
over $22,750 to $55,100	$3,413 + 28% of the amount over $22,750
over $55,100 to $115,000	$12,471 + 31% of the amount over $55,100
over $115,000 to $250,000	$31,040 + 36% of the amount over $115,000
over $250,000	$79,640 + 39.6% of the amount over $250,000

Statutory Marginal Income Tax Rates, Head-of-Household Returns	
If *taxable income* is:	Then, *tax* is:
$0 to $30,500	15% of the amount over $0
over $30,500 to $78,700	$4,575 + 28% of the amount over $30,500
over $78,700 to $127,500	$18,071 + 31% of the amount over $78,750
over $127,500 to $250,000	$33,199 + 36% of the amount over $127,500
over $250,000	$77,299 + 39.6% of the amount over $250,000

Table 10. Personal Exemptions, Standard Deductions, and Statutory Tax Rates, 1995

Personal Exemptions	$2,500

Standard Deductions	
Joint	$6,550
Single	$3,900
Head of Household	$5,750

Additional Standard Deductions for the Elderly or the Blind	
Joint	$750
Single/Head of Household	$950

Statutory Marginal Income Tax Rates, Joint Returns	
If *taxable income* is:	Then, *tax* is:
$0 to $39,000	15% of the amount over $0
over $39,000 to $94,250	$5,850 + 28% of the amount over $39,000
over $94,250 to $143,600	$21,320 + 31% of the amount over $94,250
over $143,600 to $256,500	$36,619 + 36% of the amount over $143,600
over $256,500	$77,263 + 39.6% of the amount over $256,500

Statutory Marginal Income Tax Rates, Single Returns	
If *taxable income* is:	Then, *tax* is:
$0 to $23,350	15% of the amount over $0
over $23,350 to $56,550	$3,503 + 28% of the amount over $23,350
over $56,550 to $117,950	$12,799 + 31% of the amount over $56,550
over $117,950 to $256,500	$31,833 + 36% of the amount over $117,950
over $256,500	$81,711 + 39.6% of the amount over $256,500

Statutory Marginal Income Tax Rates, Head-of-Household Returns	
If *taxable income* is:	Then, *tax* is:
$0 to $31,250	15% of the amount over $0
over $31,250 to $80,750	$4,688 + 28% of the amount over $31,250
over $80,750 to $130,800	$18,548 + 31% of the amount over $80,750
over $130,800 to $256,500	$34,063 + 36% of the amount over $130,800
over $256,500	$79,315 + 39.6% of the amount over $256,500

Table 11. Personal Exemptions, Standard Deductions, and Statutory Tax Rates, 1996

Personal Exemptions	$2,550

Standard Deductions	
Joint	$6,700
Single	$4,000
Head of Household	$5,900

Additional Standard Deductions for the Elderly or the Blind	
Joint	$800
Single/Head of Household	$1,000

Statutory Marginal Income Tax Rates, Joint Returns

If *taxable income* is:	Then, *tax* is:
$0 to $40,100	15% of the amount over $0
over $40,100 to $96,900	$6,015 + 28% of the amount over $40,100
over $96,900 to $147,700	$21,919 + 31% of the amount over $96,900
over $147,700 to $263,750	$37,667 + 36% of the amount over $147,700
over $263,750	$79,445 + 39.6% of the amount over $263,750

Statutory Marginal Income Tax Rates, Single Returns

If *taxable income* is:	Then, *tax* is:
$0 to $24,000	15% of the amount over $0
over $24,000 to $58,150	$3,600 + 28% of the amount over $24,000
over $58,150 to $121,300	$13,162 + 31% of the amount over $58,150
over $121,300 to $263,750	$32,739 + 36% of the amount over $121,300
over $263,750	$84,021 + 39.6% of the amount over $263,750

Statutory Marginal Income Tax Rates, Head-of-Household Returns

If *taxable income* is:	Then, *tax* is:
$0 to $32,150	15% of the amount over $0
over $32,150 to $83,050	$4,823 + 28% of the amount over $32,150
over $83,050 to $134,500	$19,075 + 31% of the amount over $83,050
over $134,500 to $263,750	$35,025 + 36% of the amount over $134,500
over $263,750	$81,555 + 39.6% of the amount over $263,750

Table 12. Personal Exemptions, Standard Deductions, and Statutory Tax Rates, 1997

Personal Exemptions	$2,650

Standard Deductions	
Joint	$6,900
Single	$4,150
Head of Household	$6,050

Additional Standard Deductions for the Elderly or the Blind	
Joint	$800
Single/Head of Household	$1,000

Statutory Marginal Income Tax Rates, Joint Returns

If *taxable income* is:	Then, *tax* is:
$0 to $41,200	15% of the amount over $0
over $41,200 to $99,600	$6,180 + 28% of the amount over $41,200
over $99,600 to $151,750	$22,532 + 31% of the amount over $99,600
over $151,750 to $271,050	$38,699 + 36% of the amount over $151,750
over $271,050	$81,647 + 39.6% of the amount over $271,050

Statutory Marginal Income Tax Rates, Single Returns

If *taxable income* is:	Then, *tax* is:
$0 to $ 24,650	15% of the amount over $0
over $24,650 to $ 59,750	$3,698 + 28% of the amount over $24,650
over $59,750 to $ 124,650	$13,526 + 31% of the amount over $59,750
over $124,650 to $ 271,050	$33,645 + 36% of the amount over $124,650
over $271,050	$86,349 + 39.6% of the amount over $271,050

Statutory Marginal Income Tax Rates, Head-of-Household Returns

If *taxable income* is:	Then, *tax* is:
$0 to $33,050	15% of the amount over $0
over $33,050 to $83,350	$4,958 + 28% of the amount over $33,050
over $83,350 to $138,200	$19,602 + 31% of the amount over $85,350
over $138,200 to $271,050	$35,986 + 36% of the amount over $138,200
over $271,050	$83,812 + 39.6% of the amount over $271,050

Table 13. Personal Exemptions, Standard Deductions, and Statutory Tax Rates, 1998

Personal Exemptions	$2,700
Standard Deductions	
Joint	$7,100
Single	$4,250
Head of Household	$6,250
Additional Standard Deductions for the Elderly or the Blind	
Joint	$850
Single/Head of Household	$1,050

Statutory Marginal Income Tax Rates, Joint Returns

If *taxable income* is:	Then, *tax* is:
$0 to $42,350	15% of the amount over $0
over $42,350 to $102,300	$6,353 + 28% of the amount over $42,350
over $102,300 to $155,950	$23,139 + 31% of the amount over $102,300
over $155,950 to $278,450	$39,770 + 36% of the amount over $155,950
over $278,450	$83,870 + 39.6% of the amount over $278,450

Statutory Marginal Income Tax Rates, Single Returns

If *taxable income* is:	Then, *tax* is:
$0 to $25,350	15% of the amount over $0
over $25,350 to $61,400	$3,803 + 28% of the amount over $25,350
over $61,400 to $128,100	$13,897 + 31% of the amount over $61,400
over $128,100 to $278,450	$34,574 + 36% of the amount over $128,100
over $278,450	$88,700 + 39.6% of the amount over $278,450

Statutory Marginal Income Tax Rates, Head-of-Household Returns

If *taxable income* is:	Then, *tax* is:
$0 to $33,950	15% of the amount over $0
over $33,950 to $87,700	$5,093 + 28% of the amount over $33,950
over $87,700 to $142,000	$20,143 + 31% of the amount over $87,700
over $142,000 to $278,450	$36,976+ 36% of the amount over $142,000
over $278,450	$86,098 + 39.6% of the amount over $278,450

Table 14. Personal Exemptions, Standard Deductions, and Statutory Tax Rates, 1999

Personal Exemptions	$2,750

Standard Deductions	
Joint	$7,200
Single	$4,300
Head of Household	$6,350

Additional Standard Deductions for the Elderly or the Blind	
Joint	$850
Single/Head of Household	$1,050

Statutory Marginal Income Tax Rates, Joint Returns

If *taxable income* is:	Then, *tax* is:
$0 to $43,050	15% of the amount over $0
over $43,050 to $104,050	$6,458 + 28% of the amount over $43,050
over $104,050 to $158,550	$23,538 + 31% of the amount over $104,050
over $158,550 to $283,150	$40,433 + 36% of the amount over $158,550
over $283,150	$85,289 + 39.6% of the amount over $283,150

Statutory Marginal Income Tax Rates, Single Returns

If *taxable income* is:	Then, *tax* is:
$0 to $25,750	15% of the amount over $0
over $25,750 to $62,450	$3,863 + 28% of the amount over $25,750
over $62,450 to $130,250	$14,139 + 31% of the amount over $62,450
over $130,250 to $283,150	$35,157 + 36% of the amount over $130,250
over $283,150	$90,201 + 39.6% of the amount over $283,150

Statutory Marginal Income Tax Rates, Head-of-Household Returns

If *taxable income* is:	Then, *tax* is:
$0 to $34,550	15% of the amount over $0
over $34,550 to $89,150	$5,183 + 28% of the amount over $34,550
over $89,150 to $144,400	$20,471 + 31% of the amount over $89,150
over $144,400 to $283,150	$37,598 + 36% of the amount over $144,440
over $283,150	$87,548 + 39.6% of the amount over $283,150

Table 15. Personal Exemptions, Standard Deductions, and Statutory Tax Rates, 2000

Personal Exemptions	$2,800

Standard Deductions	
Joint	$7,350
Single	$4,400
Head of Household	$6,450

Additional Standard Deductions for the Elderly or the Blind	
Joint	$850
Single/Head of Household	$1,100

Statutory Marginal Income Tax Rates, Joint Returns	
If *taxable income* is:	Then, *tax* is:
$0 to $43,850	15% of the amount over $0
over $43,850 to $105,950	$6,578 + 28% of the amount over $43,850
over $105,950 to $161,450	$23,966 + 31% of the amount over $105,950
over $161,450 to $288,350	$41,171 + 36% of the amount over $161,450
over $288,350	$86,855 + 39.6% of the amount over $288,350

Statutory Marginal Income Tax Rates, Single Returns	
If *taxable income* is:	Then, *tax* is:
$0 to $26,250	15% of the amount over $0
over $26,250 to $63,550	$3,938 + 28% of the amount over $26,250
over $63,550 to $132,600	$14,382 + 31% of the amount over $63,550
over $132,600 to $288,350	$35,787 + 36% of the amount over $132,600
over $288,350	$91,857 + 39.6% of the amount over $288,350

Statutory Marginal Income Tax Rates, Head-of-Household Returns	
If *taxable income* is:	Then, *tax* is:
$0 to $35,150	15% of the amount over $0
over $35,150 to $90,800	$5,273 + 28% of the amount over $35,150
over $90,800 to $147,050	$20,855 + 31% of the amount over $90,800
over $147,050 to $288,350	$38,292 + 36% of the amount over $147,050
over $288,350	$89,160 + 39.6% of the amount over $288,350

Table 16. Personal Exemptions, Standard Deductions, and Statutory Tax Rates, 2001

Personal Exemptions	$2,900
Standard Deductions	
Joint	$7,600
Single	$4,550
Head of Household	$6,650
Additional Standard Deductions for the Elderly or the Blind	
Joint	$900
Single/Head of Household	$1,100

Statutory Marginal Income Tax Rates, Joint Returns

If *taxable income* is:	Then, *tax* is:
$0 to $45,200	15% of the amount over $0
over $45,200 to $109,250	$6,780 + 27.5% of the amount over $45,200
over $109,250 to $166,500	$24,394 + 30.5% of the amount over $109,250
over $166,500 to $297,350	$41,855 + 35.5% of the amount over $166,500
over $297,350	$88,307 + 39.1% of the amount over $297,350

Statutory Marginal Income Tax Rates, Single Returns

If *taxable income* is:	Then, *tax* is:
$0 to $27,050	15% of the amount over $0
over $27,050 to $65,550	$4,058 + 27.5% of the amount over $27,050
over $65,550 to $136,750	$14,646 + 30.5% of the amount over $65,550
over $136,750 to $297,350	$36,362 + 35.5% of the amount over $136,750
over $297,350	$93,375 + 39.1% of the amount over $297,350

Statutory Marginal Income Tax Rates, Head-of-Household Returns

If *taxable income* is:	Then, *tax* is:
$0 to $36,250	15% of the amount over $0
over $36,250 to $93,650	$5,438 + 27.5% of the amount over $36,250
over $93,650 to $151,650	$21,223 + 30.5% of the amount over $93,650
over $151,650 to $297,350	$38,913 + 35.5% of the amount over $151,650
over $297,350	$90,637 + 39.1% of the amount over $297,350

Table 17. Personal Exemptions and Standard Deductions, 2002

Personal Exemptions	$3,000
Standard Deductions:	
Joint	$7,850
Single	$4,700
Head of Household	$6,900
Additional Standard Deductions for the Elderly or the Blind:	
Joint	$900
Single/Head of Household	$1,150

Table 18. Statutory Marginal Tax Rates, 2002

Joint Returns

If *taxable income* is:			Then, *tax* is:
$0 to	to	$12,000	10% of the amount over $0
over $12,000	to	$46,700	$1,200 + 15% of the amount over $12,000
over $46,700	to	$112,850	$6,405 + 27% of the amount over $46,700
over $112,850	to	$171,950	$24,266 + 30% of the amount over $112,850
over $171,950	to	$307,050	$41,996 + 35% of the amount over $171,950
over $307,050			$89,281 + 38.6% of the amount over $307,050

Single Returns

If *taxable income* is:			Then, *tax* is:
$0	to	$6,000	10% of the amount over $0
over $6,000	to	$27,950	$600 + 15% of the amount over $6,000
over $27,950	to	$67,700	$3,893 + 27% of the amount over $27,950
over $67,700	to	$141,250	$14,626 + 30% of the amount over $67,700
over $141,250	to	$307,050	$36,691 + 35% of the amount over $141,250
over $307,050			$94,721 + 38.6% of the amount over $307,050

Head-of-Household Returns

If *taxable income* is:			Then, *tax* is:
$0	to	$10,000	10% of the amount over $0
over $10,000	to	$37,450	$1,000 + 15% of the amount over $10,000
over $37,450	to	$96,700	$5,118 + 27% of the amount over $37,450
over $96,700	to	$156,600	$21,116 + 30% of the amount over $96,700
over $156,600	to	$307,050	$39,086 + 35% of the amount over $156,600
over $307,050			$91,744 + 38.6% of the amount over $307,050

Table 19. Statutory Marginal Tax Rates, 2003 Under Prior Law
(prior to enactment of the Jobs and Growth Tax Relief Reconciliation Act)

Joint Returns

If *taxable income* is:			Then, *tax* is:
$0	to	$12,000	10% of the amount over $0
over $12,000	to	$47,450	$1,200 + 15% of the amount over $12,000
over $47,450	to	$114,650	$6,518 + 27% of the amount over $47,450
over $114,650	to	$174,700	$24,662 + 30% of the amount over $114,650
over $174,700	to	$311,950	$42,677 + 35% of the amount over $174,700
over $311,950			$90,714 + 38.6% of the amount over $311,950

Standard Deduction for a joint return was $7,950

Single Returns

If *taxable income* is:			Then, *tax* is:
$0	to	$6,000	10% of the amount over $0
over $6,000	to	$28,400	$600 + 15% of the amount over $6,000
over $28,400	to	$68,800	$3,960 + 27% of the amount over $28,400
over $68,800	to	$143,500	$14,868 + 30% of the amount over $68,800
over $143,500	to	$311,950	$37,278 + 35% of the amount over $143,500
over $311,950			$96,236 + 38.6% of the amount over $311,950

Standard deduction for a single return is $4,750

Head-of-Household Returns

If *taxable income* is:			Then, *tax* is:
$0	to	$10,000	10% of the amount over $0
over $10,000	to	$38,050	$1,000 + 15% of the amount over $10,000
over $38,050	to	$98,250	$5,208 + 27% of the amount over $38,050
over $98,250	to	$159,100	$21,462 + 30% of the amount over $98,250
over $159,100	to	$311,950	$39,717 + 35% of the amount over $159,100
over $311,950			$93,214 + 38.6% of the amount over $311,950

Standard deduction for head of household return is $7,000

Table 20. Personal Exemptions and Standard Deductions, Limitation on Itemized Deductions, and the Personal Exemption Phaseout, 2003

(after enactment of the Jobs and Growth Tax Relief Reconciliation Act)

Personal Exemptions	$3,050
Standard Deductions:	
Joint	$9,500
Single	$4,750
Head of Household	$7,000
Additional Standard Deductions for the Elderly or the Blind and Limitation on Itemized Deductions:	
Joint	$950
Single/Head of Household	$1,150
Limitation on itemized deductions:	$139,500
Phaseout of Personal Exemptions:	
Joint	$209,250
Head of household	$174,400
Single	$139,500

Table 21. Statutory Marginal Income Tax Rates, 2003

(after enactment of the Jobs and Growth Tax Relief Reconciliation Act)

Joint Returns				
If *taxable income* is:			Then, *tax* is:	
$0	to	$14,000	10% of the amount over $0	
over $14,000	to	$56,800	$1,400 + 15% of the amount over $14,000	
over $56,800	to	$114,650	$7,820 + 25% of the amount over $56,800	
over $114,650	to	$174,700	$22,283 + 28% of the amount over $114,650	
over $174,700	to	$311,950	$39,097 + 33% of the amount over $174,700	
over $311,950			$84,390 + 35% of the amount over $311,950	

Single Returns				
If *taxable income* is:			Then, *tax* is:	
$0	to	$7,000	10% of the amount over $0	
over $7,000	to	$28,400	$700 + 15% of the amount over $7,000	
over $28,400	to	$68,800	$3,910 + 25% of the amount over $28,400	
over $68,800	to	$143,500	$14,010 + 28% of the amount over $68,800	
over $143,500	to	$311,950	$34,926 + 33% of the amount over $143,500	
over $311,950			$90,515 + 35% of the amount over $311,950	

Head-of-Household Returns			
If *taxable income* is:			Then, *tax* is:
$0	to	$10,000	10% of the amount over $0
over $10,000	to	$38,050	$1,000 + 15% of the amount over $10,000
over $38,050	to	$98,250	$5,208 + 25% of the amount over $38,050
over $98,250	to	$159,100	$20,258 + 28% of the amount over $98,250
over $159,100	to	$311,950	$37,296 + 33% of the amount over $159,100
over $311,950			$87,737 + 35% of the amount over $311,950

Table 22. Personal Exemptions and Standard Deductions, Limitation on Itemized Deductions, and the Personal Exemption Phaseout, 2004

Personal Exemptions	$3,100
Standard Deductions:	
Joint	$9,700
Single	$4,850
Head of Household	$7,150
Additional Standard Deductions for the Elderly or the Blind and Limitation on Itemized Deductions:	
Joint	$950
Single/Head of Household	$1,200
Limitation on itemized deductions:	$142,700
Phaseout of Personal Exemptions:	
Joint	$214,050
Head of household	$178,350
Single	$142,700

Table 23. Statutory Marginal Income Tax Rates, 2004

Joint Returns			
If *taxable income* is:			Then, *tax* is:
$ 0	to	$14,300	10% of the amount over $0
over $14,300	to	$58,100	$1,430 + 15% of the amount over $14,300
over $58,100	to	$117,250	$8,000 + 25% of the amount over $58,100
over $117,250	to	$178,650	$22,788 + 28% of the amount over $117,250
over $178,650	to	$319,100	$39,980 + 33% of the amount over $178,650
over $319,100			$86,328 + 35% of the amount over $319,100

Single Returns			
If *taxable income* is:			Then, *tax* is:
$0	to	$7,150	10% of the amount over $0
over $7,150	to	$29,050	$715 + 15% of the amount over $7,150
over $29,050	to	$70,350	$4,000 + 25% of the amount over $29,050
over $70,350	to	$146,750	$14,325 + 28% of the amount over $70,350
over $146,750	to	$319,100	$35,717 + 33% of the amount over $146,750
over $319,100			$92,593 + 35% of the amount over $319,100

Head-of-Household Returns			
If *taxable income* is:			Then, *tax* is:
$0	to	$10,200	10% of the amount over $0
over $10,200	to	$38,900	$1,020 + 15% of the amount over $10,200
over $38,900	to	$100,500	$5,325 + 25% of the amount over $38,900
over $100,500	to	$162,700	$20,725 + 28% of the amount over $100,500
over $162,700	to	$319,100	$38,141 + 33% of the amount over $162,700
over $319,100			$89,753 + 35% of the amount over $319,100

Table 24. Personal Exemptions, Standard Deductions, Limitation on Itemized Deductions and the Personal Exemption Phaseout Thresholds, 2005

Personal Exemptions	$3,200
Standard Deductions:	
Joint	$10,000
Single	$5,000
Head of Household	$7,300
Additional Standard Deductions for the Elderly or the Blind and Limitation on Itemized Deductions:	
Joint (each spouse)	$1,000
Single/Head of Household	$1,250
Limitation on itemized deductions:	$145,950
Phaseout of Personal Exemptions:	
Joint	$218,950
Head of household	$182,450
Single	$145,950

Table 25. Statutory Marginal Income Tax Rates, 2005

Joint Returns			
If *taxable income* is:			Then, *tax* is:
$0	to	$14,600	10% of the amount over $0
over $14,600	to	$59,400	$1,460 + 15% of the amount over $14,600
over $59,400	to	$119,950	$8,180 + 25% of the amount over $59,400
over $119,950	to	$182,800	$23,318 + 28% of the amount over $119,950
over $182,800	to	$326,450	$40,916 + 33% of the amount over $182,800
over $326,450			$88,321 + 35% of the amount over $326,450

Single Returns			
If *taxable income* is:			Then, *tax* is:
$0	to	$7,300	10% of the amount over $0
over $7,300	to	$29,700	$730 + 15% of the amount over $7,300
over $29,700	to	$71,950	$4,090 + 25% of the amount over $29,700
over $71,950	to	$150,150	$14,653 + 28% of the amount over $71,950
over $150,150	to	$326,450	$36,549 + 33% of the amount over $150,150
over $326,450			$94,728 + 35% of the amount over $326,450

Head-of-Household Returns			
If *taxable income* is:			Then, *tax* is:
$0	to	$10,450	10% of the amount over $0
over $10,450	to	$39,800	$1,045 + 15% of the amount over $10,450
over $39,800	to	$102,800	$5,448 + 25% of the amount over $39,800
over $102,800	to	$166,450	$21,198 + 28% of the amount over $102,800
over $166,450	to	$326,450	$39,020 + 33% of the amount over $166,450
over $326,450			$91,820 + 35% of the amount over $326,450

Table 26. Personal Exemptions, Standard Deductions, Limitation on Itemized Deductions and the Personal Exemption Phaseout Thresholds, 2006

Personal Exemptions	$3,300
Standard Deductions:	
Joint	$10,300
Single	$5,150
Head of Household	$7,550
Additional Standard Deductions for the Elderly or the Blind and Limitation on Itemized Deductions:	
Joint (each spouse)	$1,000
Single/Head of Household	$1,250
Limitation on itemized deductions:	$150,500
Phaseout of Personal Exemptions:	
Joint	$225,750
Head of household	$188,150
Single	$150,500

Table 27. Statutory Marginal Income Tax Rates, 2006

Joint Returns			
If *taxable income* is:			Then, *tax* is:
$0	to	$15,100	10% of the amount over $0
over $15,100	to	$61,300	$1,510 + 15% of the amount over $15,100
over $61,300	to	$123,700	$8,440 + 25% of the amount over $61,300
over $123,700	to	$188,450	$24,040 + 28% of the amount over $123,700
over $188,450	to	$336,550	$42,170 + 33% of the amount over $188,450
over $336,550			$91,043 + 35% of the amount over $336,550

Single Returns			
If *taxable income* is:			Then, *tax* is:
$0	to	$7,550	10% of the amount over $0
over $7,550	to	$30,650	$755 + 15% of the amount over $7,550
over $30,650	to	$74,200	$4,220 + 25% of the amount over $30,650
over $74,200	to	$154,800	$15,108 + 28% of the amount over $74,200
over $154,800	to	$336,550	$37,676 + 33% of the amount over $154,800
over $336,550			$97,653 + 35% of the amount over $336,550

Head-of-Household Returns			
If *taxable income* is:			Then, *tax* is:
$0	to	$10,750	10% of the amount over $0
over $10,750	to	$41,050	$1,075 + 15% of the amount over $10,750
over $41,050	to	$106,000	$5,620 + 25% of the amount over $41,050
over $106,000	to	$171,650	$21,858 + 28% of the amount over $106,000
over $171,650	to	$336,550	$40,240 + 33% of the amount over $171,650
over $336,550			$94,657 + 35% of the amount over $336,550

Table 28. Personal Exemptions, Standard Deductions, Limitation on Itemized Deductions and the Personal Exemption Phaseout Thresholds, 2007

Personal Exemptions	$3,400
Standard Deductions:	
Joint	$10,700
Single	$5,350
Head of Household	$7,850
Additional Standard Deductions for the Elderly or the Blind:	
Joint (each spouse)	$1,050
Single/Head of Household	$1,300
Limitation on itemized deductions:	$156,400
Phaseout of Personal Exemptions:	
Joint	$234,600
Head of household	$195,500
Single	$156,400

Table 29. Statutory Marginal Income Tax Rates, 2007

Joint Returns			
If *taxable income* is:			Then, *tax* is:
$0	to	$15,650	10% of the amount over $0
over $15,650	to	$63,700	$1,565 + 15% of the amount over $15,650
over $63,700	to	$128,500	$8,773 + 25% of the amount over $63,700
over $128,500	to	$195,850	$24,973 + 28% of the amount over $128,500
over $195,850	to	$349,700	$43,831 + 33% of the amount over $195,850
over $349,700			$94,601 + 35% of the amount over $349,700
Single Returns			
If *taxable income* is:			Then, *tax* is:
$0	to	$7,825	10% of the amount over $0
over $7,825	to	$31,850	$783 + 15% of the amount over $7,825
over $31,850	to	$77,100	$4,386 + 25% of the amount over $31,850
over $77,100	to	$160,850	$15,699 + 28% of the amount over $77,100
over $160,850	to	$349,700	$39,149 + 33% of the amount over $160,850
over $349,700			$101,469 + 35% of the amount over $349,700

Head-of-Household Returns				
If *taxable income* is:			Then, *tax* is:	
$0	to	$11,200	10% of the amount over $0	
over $11,200	to	$42,650	$1,120 + 15% of the amount over $11,200	
over $42,650	to	$110,100	$5,838 + 25% of the amount over $42,650	
over $110,100	to	$178,350	$22,700 + 28% of the amount over $110,100	
over $178,350	to	$349,700	$41,810 + 33% of the amount over $178,350	
over $349,700			$98,356 + 35% of the amount over $349,700	

Table 30. Personal Exemptions, Standard Deductions, Limitation on Itemized Deductions and the Personal Exemption Phaseout Thresholds, 2008

Personal Exemptions	$3,500
Standard Deductions:	
Joint	$10,900
Single	$5,450
Head of Household	$8,000
Additional Standard Deductions for the Elderly or the Blind:	
Joint (each spouse)	$1,050
Single/Head of Household	$1,350
Limitation on itemized deductions:	$159,950
Phaseout of personal exemptions:	
Joint	$239,950
Head of household	$199,900
Single	$159,950

Table 31. Statutory Marginal Income Tax Rates, 2008

Joint Returns

If *taxable income* is:			Then, *tax* is:
$0	to	$16,050	10% of the amount over $0
over $16,050	to	$65,100	$1,605 + 15% of the amount over $16,050
over $65,100	to	$131,450	$8,962.50 + 25% of the amount over $65,100
over $131,450	to	$200,300	$25,550 + 28% of the amount over $131,450
over $200,300	to	$357,700	$44,828 + 33% of the amount over $200,300
over $357,700			$96,770 + 35% of the amount over $357,700

Single Returns

If *taxable income* is:			Then, *tax* is:
$0	to	$8,025	10% of the amount over $0
over $8,025	to	$32,550	$802.50 + 15% of the amount over $8,025
over $32,550	to	$78,850	$4,481.25 + 25% of the amount over $32,550
over $78,850	to	$164,550	$16,056.25 + 28% of the amount over $78,850
over $164,550	to	$357,700	$40,052.25 + 33% of the amount over $164,550
over $357,700			$103,791.75 + 35% of the amount over $357,700

Head-of-Household Returns

If *taxable income* is:			Then, *tax* is:
$0	to	$11,450	10% of the amount over $0
over $11,450	to	$43,650	$1,145 + 15% of the amount over $11,450
over $43,650	to	$112,650	$5,975 + 25% of the amount over $43,650
over $112,650	to	$182,400	$23,225 + 28% of the amount over $112,650
over $182,400	to	$357,700	$42,755 + 33% of the amount over $182,400
over $357,700			$100,604 + 35% of the amount over $357,700

Table 32. Personal Exemptions, Standard Deductions, Limitation on Itemized Deductions and the Personal Exemption Phaseout Thresholds, 2009

Personal Exemptions	$3,650
Standard Deductions:	
Joint	$11,400
Single	$5,700
Head of Household	$8,350
Additional Standard Deductions for the Elderly or the Blind:	
Joint (each spouse)	$1,100
Single/Head of Household	$1,400
Limitation on itemized deductions:	$166,800
Phaseout of personal exemptions:	
Joint	$250,200
Head of household	$208,500
Single	$166,800

Table 33. Statutory Marginal Income Tax Rates, 2009

Joint Returns			
If *taxable income* is:			Then, *tax* is:
$0	to	$16,700	10% of the amount over $0
over $16,700	to	$67,900	$1,670 + 15% of the amount over $16,700
over $67,900	to	$137,050	$9,350 + 25% of the amount over $67,900
over $137,050	to	$208,850	$26,637.50 + 28% of the amount over $137,050
over $208,850	to	$372,950	$46,741.50 + 33% of the amount over $208,850
over $372,950			$100,894.50 + 35% of the amount over $372,950
Single Returns			
If *taxable income* is:			Then, *tax* is:
$0	to	$8,350	10% of the amount over $0
over $8,350	to	$33,950	$835 + 15% of the amount over $8,350
over $33,950	to	$82,250	$4,675 + 25% of the amount over $33,950
over $82,250	to	$171,550	$16,750 + 28% of the amount over $82,250
over $171,550	to	$372,950	$41,754 + 33% of the amount over $171,550
over $372,950			$108,216 + 35% of the amount over $372,950

Head-of-Household Returns			
If *taxable income* is:			Then, *tax* is:
$0	to	$11,950	10% of the amount over $0
over $11,950	to	$45,500	$1,195 + 15% of the amount over $11,950
over $45,500	to	$117,450	$6,227.50 + 25% of the amount over $45,500
over $117,450	to	$190,200	$24,215 + 28% of the amount over $117,450
over $190,200	to	$372,950	$44,585 + 33% of the amount over $190,200
over $372,950			$104,892.50 + 35% of the amount over $372,950

Table 34. Personal Exemptions, Standard Deductions, Limitation on Itemized Deductions, and the Personal Exemption Phaseout Thresholds, 2010

Personal Exemptions	$3,650
Standard Deductions:	
Joint	$11,400
Single	$5,700
Head of Household	$8,400
Additional Standard Deductions for the Elderly or the Blind:	
Joint (each spouse)	$1,100
Single/Head of Household	$1,400
Limitation on itemized deductions:	Terminated on Dec. 31, 2009
Phaseout of personal exemptions:	
Joint	Terminated on Dec. 31, 2009
Head of household	Terminated on Dec. 31, 2009
Single	Terminated on Dec. 31, 2009

Table 35. Statutory Marginal Income Tax Rates, 2010

Joint Returns			
If *taxable income* is:			Then, *tax* is:
$0	to	$16,750	10% of the amount over $0
over $16,750	to	$68,000	$1,675 + 15% of the amount over $16,750
over $68,000	to	$137,300	$9,362.50 + 25% of the amount over $68,000
over $137,300	to	$209,250	$26,687.50 + 28% of the amount over $137,300
over $209,250	to	$373,650	$46,833.50 + 33% of the amount over $209,250
over $373,650			$100,894.50 + 35% of the amount over $373,650

Single Returns

If *taxable income* is:			Then, *tax* is:
$0	to	$8,375	10% of the amount over $0
over $8,375	to	$34,000	$837.50 + 15% of the amount over $8,375
over $34,000	to	$82,400	$4,681.25 + 25% of the amount over $34,000
over $82,400	to	$171,850	$16,781.25 + 28% of the amount over $82,400
over $171,850	to	$373,650	$41,827.25 + 33% of the amount over $171,850
over $373,650			$108,421.25 + 35% of the amount over $373,650

Head-of-Household Returns

If *taxable income* is:			Then, *tax* is:
$0	to	$11,950	10% of the amount over $0
over $11,950	to	$45,550	$1,195 + 15% of the amount over $11,950
over $45,550	to	$117,650	$6,235 + 25% of the amount over $45,550
over $117,650	to	$190,550	$24,215 + 28% of the amount over $117,650
over $190,550	to	$373,650	$44,672 + 33% of the amount over $190,550
over $373,650			$105,095 + 35% of the amount over $373,650

Table 36. Personal Exemptions, Standard Deductions, Limitation on Itemized Deductions, and the Personal Exemption Phaseout Thresholds, 2011

Personal Exemptions	$3,700
Standard Deductions:	
Joint	$11,600
Single	$5,800
Head of Household	$8,500
Additional Standard Deduction for the Elderly or the Blind:	
Joint (each spouse)	$1,150
Single/Head of Household	$1,450
Limitation on itemized deductions:	Terminated on Dec. 31, 2009
Phaseout of personal exemptions:	
Joint	Terminated on Dec. 31, 2009
Head of household	Terminated on Dec. 31, 2009
Single	Terminated on Dec. 31, 2009

Table 37. Statutory Marginal Income Tax Rates, 2011

Joint Returns

If *taxable income* is:			Then, *tax* is:
$ 0	to	$17,000	10% of the amount over $0
over $17,000	to	$69,000	$1,700 + 15% of the amount over $17,000
over $69,000	to	$139,350	$9,.500 + 25% of the amount over $69,000
over $139,350	to	$212,300	$27,087.50 + 28% of the amount over $139,350
over $212,300	to	$379,150	$47,513.50 + 33% of the amount over $212,300
over $379,150			$102,574 + 35% of the amount over $379,150

Single Returns

If *taxable income* is:			Then, *tax* is:
$0	to	$8,500	10% of the amount over $0
over $8,500	to	$34,500	$850 + 15% of the amount over $8,500
over $34,500	to	$83,600	$4,750 + 25% of the amount over $34,500
over $83,600	to	$174,400	$17,025 + 28% of the amount over $83,600
over $174,400	to	$379,150	$42,449 + 33% of the amount over $174,400
over $379,150			$110,016.50 + 35% of the amount over $379,150

Head-of-Household Returns

If *taxable income* is:			Then, *tax* is:
$0	to	$12,150	10% of the amount over $0
over $12,150	to	$46,250	$1,215 + 15% of the amount over $12,150
over $46,250	to	$119,400	$6,330 + 25% of the amount over $46,250
over $119,400	to	$193,350	$24,617.50 + 28% of the amount over $119,400
over $193,350	to	$379,150	$45,322.50 + 33% of the amount over $193,350
over $379,150			$106,637.50 + 35% of the amount over $379,150

Table 38. Personal Exemptions, Standard Deductions, Limitation on Itemized Deductions, and the Personal Exemption Phaseout Thresholds, 2012

Personal Exemptions	$3,800
Standard Deductions:	
Joint	$11,900
Single	$5,950
Head of Household	$8,700
Additional Standard Deduction for the Elderly or the Blind:	
Joint (each spouse)	$1,150
Single/Head of Household	$1,450
Limitation on itemized deductions:	Terminated on Dec. 31, 2009
Phaseout of personal exemptions:	
Joint	Terminated on Dec. 31, 2009
Head of household	Terminated on Dec. 31, 2009
Single	Terminated on Dec. 31, 2009

Table 39. Statutory Marginal Income Tax Rates, 2012

Joint Returns			
If *taxable income* is:			Then, *tax* is:
$0	to	$17,400	10% of the amount over $0
over $17,400	to	$70,700	$1,700 + 15% of the amount over $17,000
over $70,700	to	$142,700	$9,500 + 25% of the amount over $69,000
over $142,700	to	$217,450	$27,087.50 + 28% of the amount over $139,350
over $217,450	to	$388,350	$47,513.50 + 33% of the amount over $212,300
over $388,350			$102,574 + 35% of the amount over $379,150

Single Returns			
If *taxable income* is:			Then, *tax* is:
$0	to	$8,700	10% of the amount over $0
over $8,700	to	$35,350	$850 + 15% of the amount over $8,500
over $35,350	to	$85,650	$4,750 + 25% of the amount over $34,500
over $85,650	to	$178,650	$17,025 + 28% of the amount over $83,600
over $178,650	to	$388,350	$42,449 + 33% of the amount over $174,400
over $388,350			$110,016.50 + 35% of the amount over $379,150

Head-of-Household Returns				
If *taxable income* is:			Then, *tax* is:	
$0	to	$12,400	10% of the amount over $0	
over $12,400	to	$47,350	$1,215 + 15% of the amount over $12,150	
over $47,350	to	$122,300	$6,330 + 25% of the amount over $46,250	
over $122,300	to	$198,050	$24,617.50 + 28% of the amount over $119,400	
over $198,050	to	$388,350	$45,322.50 + 33% of the amount over $193,350	
over $388,350			$106,637.50 + 35% of the amount over $379,150	

Table 40. Personal Exemptions, Standard Deductions, Limitation on Itemized Deductions, and the Personal Exemption Phaseout Thresholds, 2013

Personal Exemptions	$3,900
Standard Deductions:	
Joint	$12,200
Single	$6,100
Head of Household	$8,950
Additional Standard Deduction for the Elderly or the Blind:	
Joint (each spouse)	$1,200
Single/Head of Household	$1,500
Limitation on Itemized Deductions:	Reduction in itemized deduction equal to the lesser of 3% of the excess of adjusted gross income above the following threshold amount, or 80% of the amount of itemized deductions otherwise allowable:
Joint	$300,000
Head of Household	$275,000
Single	$250,000
Phaseout of personal exemptions:	Complete phaseout occurs at the following adjusted gross incomes:
Joint	$422,501
Head of household	$397,501
Single	$372,501
Tax on Net Investment Income:	3.8% of the lesser of any excess of gross income from interest, dividends, annuities, royalties, rents, and net capital gains over allowable deductions for this income, or the amount of modified adjusted gross income above the following threshold amounts:
Joint	$250,000
Head of Household	$200,000
Single	$125,000

Table 41. Statutory Marginal Income Tax Rates, 2013

Joint Returns

If *taxable income* is:			Then, *tax* is:
$0	to	$17,850	10% of the amount over $0
over $17,850	to	$72,500	$1,785 + 15% of the amount over $17,850
over $72,500	to	$146,400	$9,982.50 + 25% of the amount over $72,500
over $146,400	to	$223,050	$28,457.50 + 28% of the amount over $146,400
over $223,050	to	$398,350	$49,919.50 + 33% of the amount over $223,050
over $398,350	to	$450,000	$107,768.50 + 35% of the amount over $398,350
over $450,000			$125,846 + 39.6% of the amount over $50,000

Single Returns

If *taxable income* is:			Then, *tax* is:
$0	to	$8,925	10% of the amount over $0
over $8,925	to	$36,250	$892.50 + 15% of the amount over $8,925
over $36,250	to	$87,850	$4,991.25 + 25% of the amount over $36,250
over $87,850	to	$183,250	$17,891.25 + 28% of the amount over $87,850
over $183,250	to	$398,350	$44,603.25 + 33% of the amount over $183,250
over $398,350	to	$400,000	$115,586.25 + 35% of the amount over $398,350
over $400,000			$116,163.75 + 39.6% of the amount over$400,000

Head-of-Household Returns

If *taxable income* is:			Then, *tax* is:
$0	to	$12,750	10% of the amount over $0
over $12,750	to	$48,600	$1,275 + 15% of the amount over $12,750
over $48,600	to	$125,450	$6,652.50 + 25% of the amount over $48,600
over $125,450	to	$203,150	$25,865 + 28% of the amount over $125,450
over $203,150	to	$398,350	$47,621 + 33% of the amount over $203,150
over $398,350	to	$425,000	$112,037 + 35% of the amount over $398,350
over $425,000			$121,364.50 + 39.6% of the amount over $425,000

Author Contact Information

Gary Guenther
Analyst in Public Finance
gguenther@crs.loc.gov, 7-7742

Acknowledgments

Greg Esenwein, a former CRS analyst, was the original author of this report. Max Shvedov, another former CRS analyst, also made significant contributions to it.

www.ingramcontent.com/pod-product-compliance
Lightning Source LLC
Chambersburg PA
CBHW081231170526
45165CB00009B/3034